Junior and Bobo
The Beach Bulldogs

Let Sleeping Dogs Lie

Roxanne Dean

DEDICATION

Bulldogs are the fourth most popular breed in the country right now.
There are logos everywhere with Bulldogs on them.
The Marine Corp Mascot is the English Bulldog.
Bulldogs have been used in famous cartoons, and service industries to promote support, strength and loyalty. They are lovable and loyal, so Enjoy!

CONTENTS

ACKNOWLEDGMENTS

Thanks to Lenore and Neil Callahan
for sharing their Bulldog experiences about Junior
and Bobo and their photos so that everyone can
enjoy them!

Bulldog Facts

1

"Don't judge a book by its cover" should be the trademark of the English Bulldog. Never has the look of a breed been so contrary to its demeanor: for under the almost-stern, always frowning face of an English Bulldog lies a warm, friendly, amiable dog!

LUCY PET

The English Bulldogs breed was specially trained for the barbaric sport of bull baiting, or attacking a bull. The dogs could fasten their

teeth in the bull's snout and it could not be shaken loose. Thus the dogs were bred to be shorter and lower to the ground so it couldn't be thrown by the bull's horns. The under bite was then developed to give the dogs more gripping power on the bull's nose and the skin folds were for the purpose of protecting the dog's eyes.

The dogs had innate stubbornness that enabled it to hold on to the bull despite physical pain.

In 1835 an Act of Congress outlawed this barbaric sport but the breed had been established.

The breed is definitely a couch potato but also the ideal companions. They are known to pass gas while sitting next to you so make sure you choose the right food for a healthy digestive system!
The breed is not a great swimmer although there have been some that proved to be the exception.

Look for the book by Roxanne Dean:
(Lenny The Bulldog Goes To The Beach)

This book is about a special bulldog who loved to swim!!

They are known to take lots of naps and can easily sleep the day away and need very little exercise. Routines are important, If the dogs know that treats are part of their walks, there will be more success in getting them out on the leash.
They don't need a lot of exercise and are generally stress-free dogs.

English Bulldogs can also be left alone for long periods of time.

Financially, most English Bulldogs are expensive with an average cost of $1000+ per puppy. So if you are interested in a "Bullie" be prepared to pay the cost. Part of this is because they are unable to conceive or give birth naturally. They are commonly bred using artificial insemination and if bred will need to have a costly C-section due to very small birth canals of the breed.

Eye cleaning is important as they are prone to eye infections due to wrinkles around their eyes. Thus, it is important to clean the eye area with a warm cloth every morning. They also tend to hide dirt and bacteria in the wrinkles so it is necessary to clean them daily with mild soap and moisturizer to avoid trips to the vet.

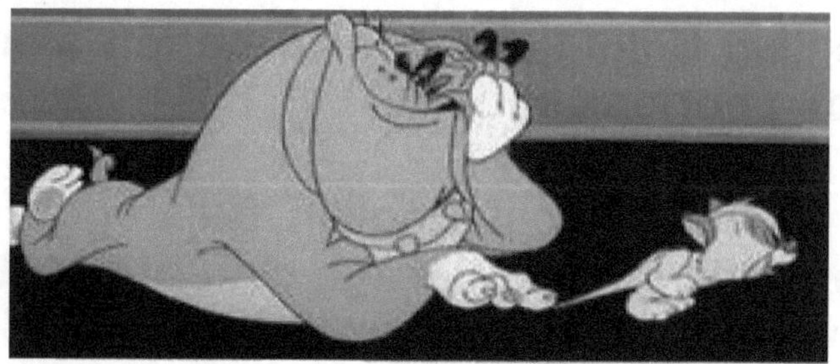

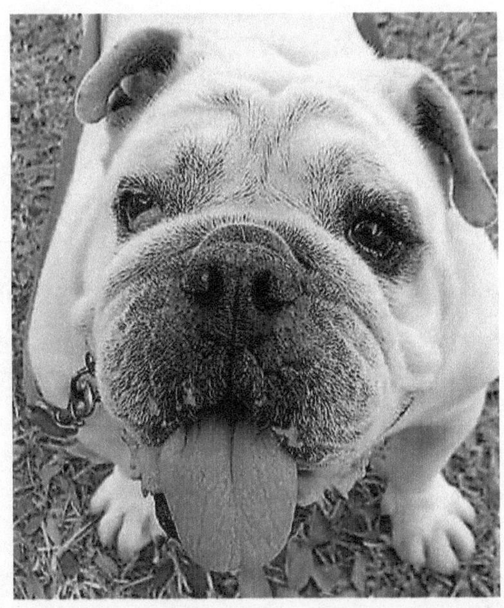

Here's a quiz about the greatest, most lovable dogs in the world, English Bulldogs

1. From which of these breeds is the modern bulldog descended?

- ○ Saint Bernard
- ○ Welsh Corgi
- ○ German shepherd
- ○ Mastiff

2. Bulldogs are known for their aggressive, vicious nature.

○ True
○ False

3. What was the name of the first bulldog registered in the Bull Dog Club in London in 1874?

○ Mike
○ Waldo
○ Spike
○ Adam

4. Which of these US Presidents had a bully?

○ Andrew Jackson
○ Chester Arthur
○ Warren Harding
○ Ronald Reagan

5. Winston Churchill owned a bulldog.

- ○ True
- ○ False

6. According to the American Kennel Club, which category are bullies grouped in?

- ○ Sporting
- ○ Hounds
- ○ Toy
- ○ Non-sporting

7. Which of these is NOT true of bulldogs?

- ○ They are known as 'sourmugs'
- ○ They are easy to care for
- ○ They are the mascot of the US Marine Corps
- ○ They are lazy

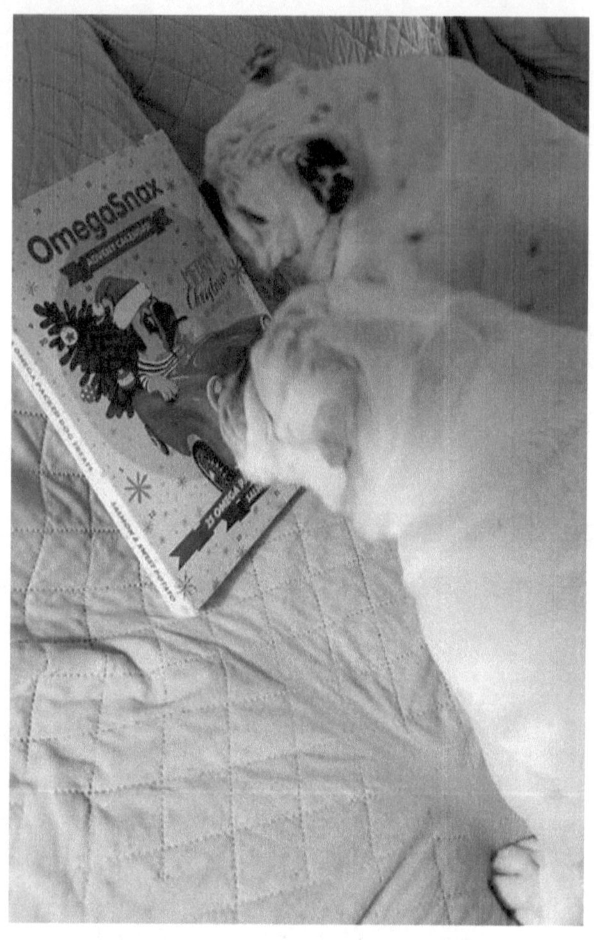
OmegaSnax

8. What's the name of the bulldog on the Kibbles and Bits commercial?

○ Frank

○ Spike

○ Ike

○ Ralph

9. French bulldogs are related to English bulldogs.

○ True

○ False

10. What college has a bully named Uga as its mascot?

○ University of Georgia

○ Penn State University

○ Duke University

○ UCLA

1. From which of these breeds is the modern bulldog descended?

 **Your Answer:** Mastiff
Today's Bulldogs, bred in England for the sport of 'bullbaiting', are descendants of the huge Mastiff and cute little Pug. (There is debate on whether the Pug was added to reduce size and make a gentler temperment). Bullbaiting was a cruel sport in which the dogs were trained to attack bulls running around a ring; fortunately, this practice was outlawed in 1835.

2. Bulldogs are known for their vicious, aggressive behavior.

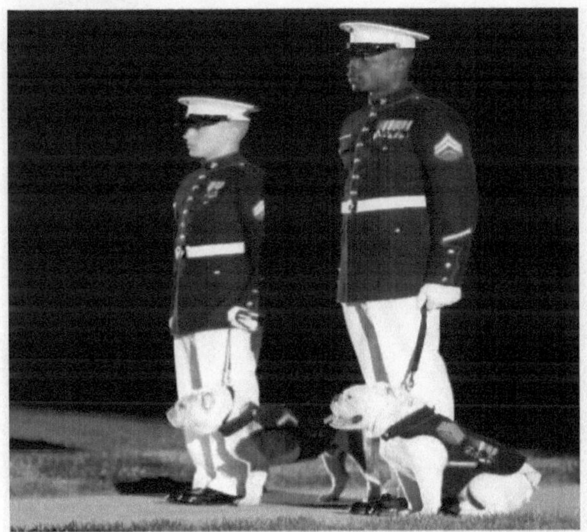

Your Answer: False

This could not be more false! Bullies

are known for their gentle, loving nature and are great with children.

3. What was the name of the first bulldog registered
 in the Bull Dog Club in London in 1874?
Your Answer: Adam

The first standard of the breed was established in 1864, and the first Bulldog Club was created 10 years later. I guess it's fitting that the first entrant was named Adam!

4. Which of these US Presidents had a bully?
Your Answer: Warren Harding

Warren Harding, who was President from 1921 to 1923,was the father of a bulldog named Oh Boy.

5. Winston Churchill owned a bulldog.

Your Answer: False
Although many people believe that the famousBritish statesman had a bully, he actually owned aPug- or at least his daughter did. When the littlegirl's Pug was sick once, Winston wrote her a poem about him in which he referred to the Pug as 'Puggy Wug'.

6. According to the American Kennel Club, which category are bullies grouped in?

Your Answer: Non-sporting
The Non-Sporting category basically contains dogs that are no longer bred for any special purpose such as hunting or working. Bullies are definitely not Toys.

7. Which of these is NOT true of bulldogs?

 **Your Answer:** They are easy to care for

Bullies are considered 'high maintenance' dogs for the amount of care they require. Their cute smashed noses make them susceptible to breathing problems and respiratory infections. They cannot tolerate heat, so if you have a bully you must have air conditioning. The folds in their thick skin must be cleaned regularly to keep them from becoming infected.

8. What's the name of the bulldog on the Kibbles and Bits commercial?

 **Your Answer:** Ike

Ike is the 'spokesbully' for Kibbles and Bits dog food (which my bully Snoopy eats). You'll see him on commercials and on the food bags.

9. French bulldogs are related to English bulldogs.

Your Answer: True
The smaller, more delicate-looking 'Frenchies' are actually descended from their bigger English cousins. In the mid-1800s terriers were mixed with English bullies to produce the smaller French specimen. Frenchies were said to be a favorite lap dog among Parisian prostitutes!

10. What college has a bully named Uga as its mascot?

Your Answer: University of Georgia
Uga is the mascot for the University of Georgia in Athens, Georgia. Actually, Uga is not one but a series of bullies by the same name.

2.

Many Sports' teams use the Bulldog as their mascot.

BULLDOG
PRIDE!

BULLDOG
BASKETBALL
gg82662884 www.gograph.com

NAVALLEY
BULLDOGS
PASA

shutterstock.com • 1215284440

History

BULLDOGS
BARBELLS

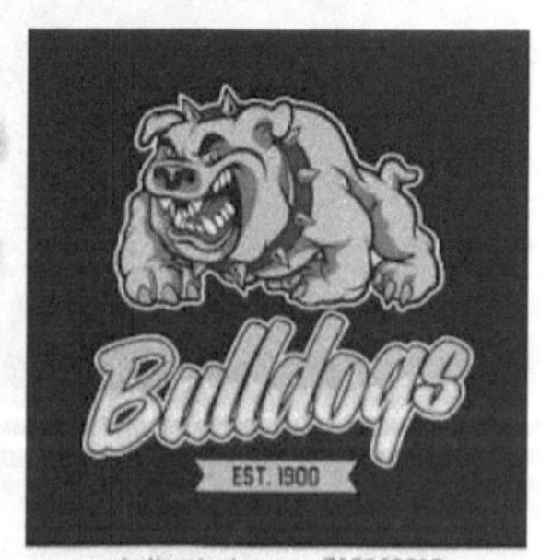

Bulldogs
EST. 1900
shutterstock.com · 713068813

BULLDOG
BASKETBALL

FLOU

STATE
BRYANT
UNIVERSITY
BULLDOGS
bulldog
BASKETBALL
© Can Stock Photo - csp18306116

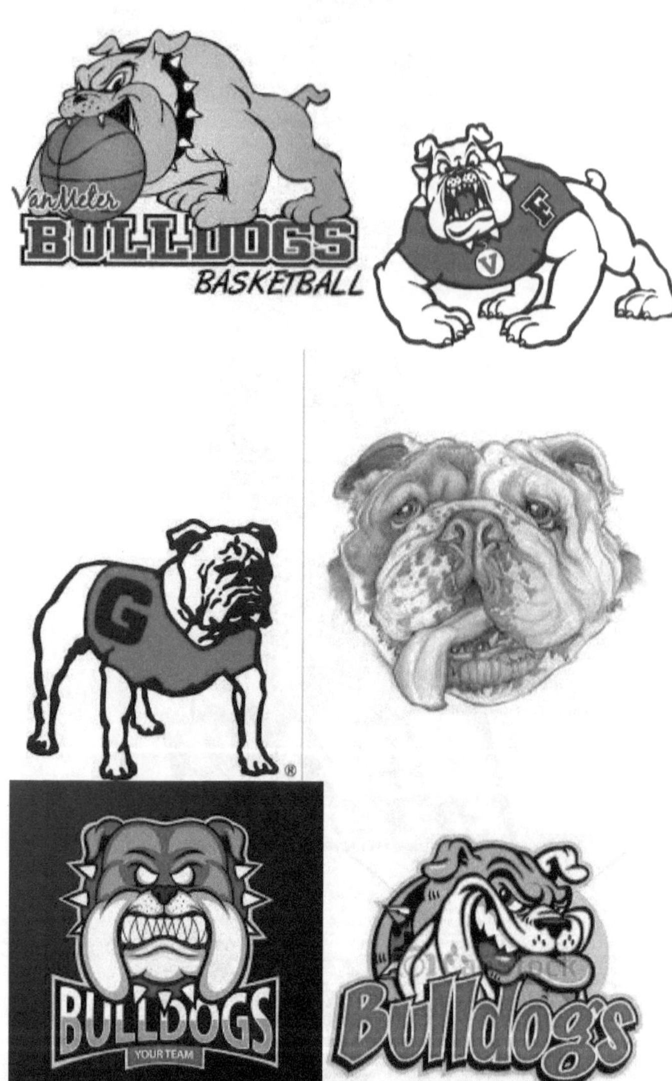

Van Meter
BULLDOGS
BASKETBALL
G
BULLDOGS
YOUR TEAM
Bulldogs
© Can Stock Photo - csp14003761

CANTERBURY-BANKSTOWN BULLDOGS

BULLDOG
SECURITY

BACKBONE
BULLDOGS
OH

MCPHERSON
COLLEGE

Discipline
Bulldog Style

Bulldog
studio

BULLDOG
PRIDE!

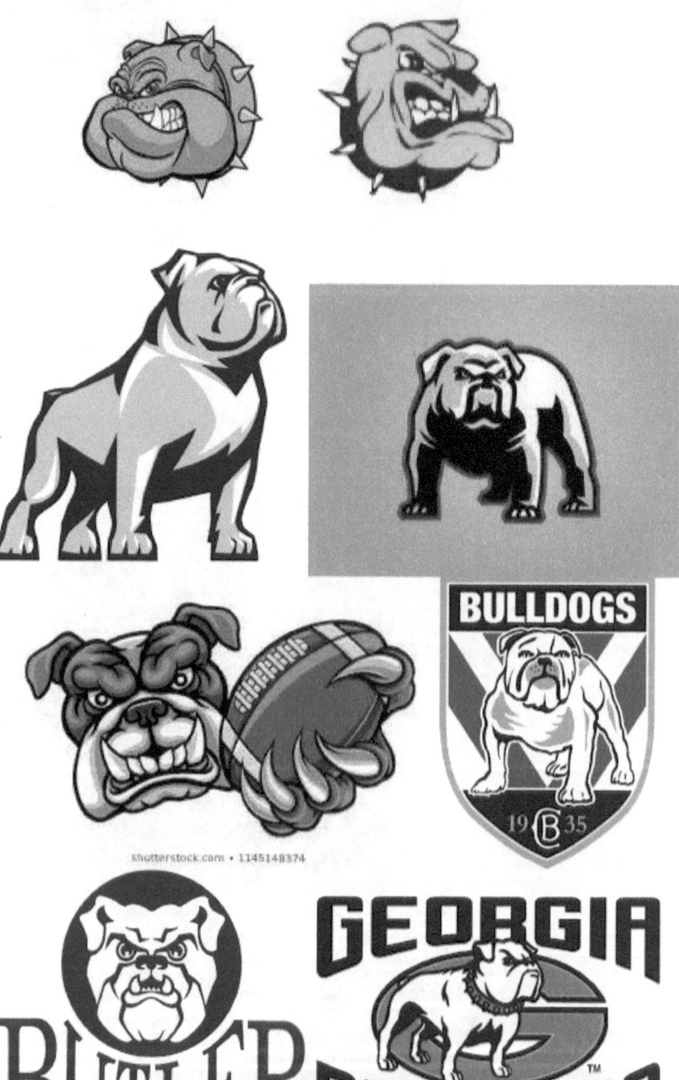

BULLDOGS
19 35
GEORGIA
BUTLER
BULLDOGS

3 Junior

Junior arrived at the Callahan's after Lenny. He soon took over their hearts. Junior was a sweetheart from the beginning. He took over the void and was a cute little puppy. He was solid white with leopard ears and freckles throughout. He could have been named spotted ears.

The Callahan's picked Junior out of a group from a local breeder. It was a good choice. He soon learned to travel in a truck and go back and forth from one beach to another. From May till October, he lived in Bethany Beach, Delaware and had lots of neighborly doggie friends and people friends.

Junior was named after a popular show called "HEEHAW" There was a character on the show named Junior. His whole name was Alvin Samples, Jr.
Alvin Samples, Jr. Junior Samples, born **Alvin Samples Jr.** (April 10, 1926 – November 13, 1983) was an American comedian best known for his 14-year run as a cast member of the TV show Hee Haw.

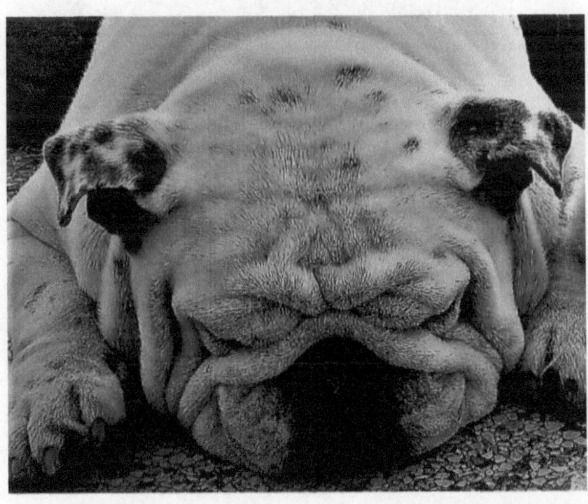

Junior looks quit handsome when he wears his Toys For Tots Marine Corp Uniform. He is the

director of this event each year around Christmastime in St. Pete's Beach, Florida.

Junior has major allergies and at five years old, now has to get allergy shots once a week. He is allergic to grass, cats, some trees etc etc. After being the only dog in the family for some time, Junior was happy to have a buddy join him. Bobo fit right into the family!

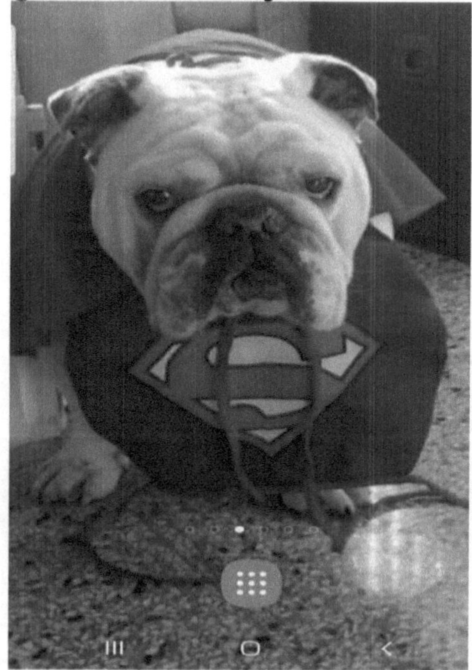

Super Junior
What a Face!!!

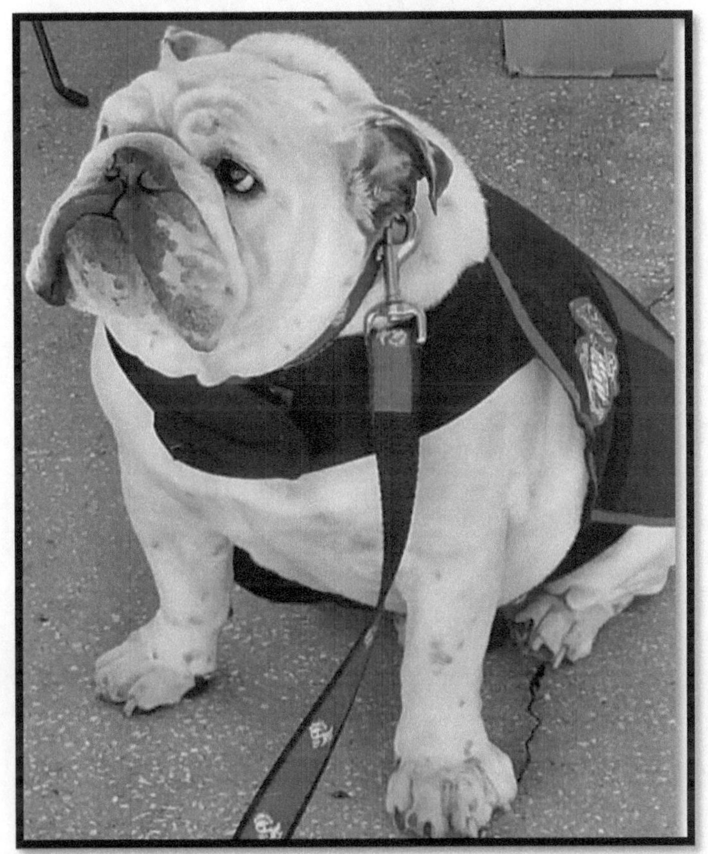

Junior is Modeling his Marine Corp Uniform

Bobo   Neil(part Bulldog)   Junior

Young Junior on his front seat spot in the truck.
Cruising the beach!

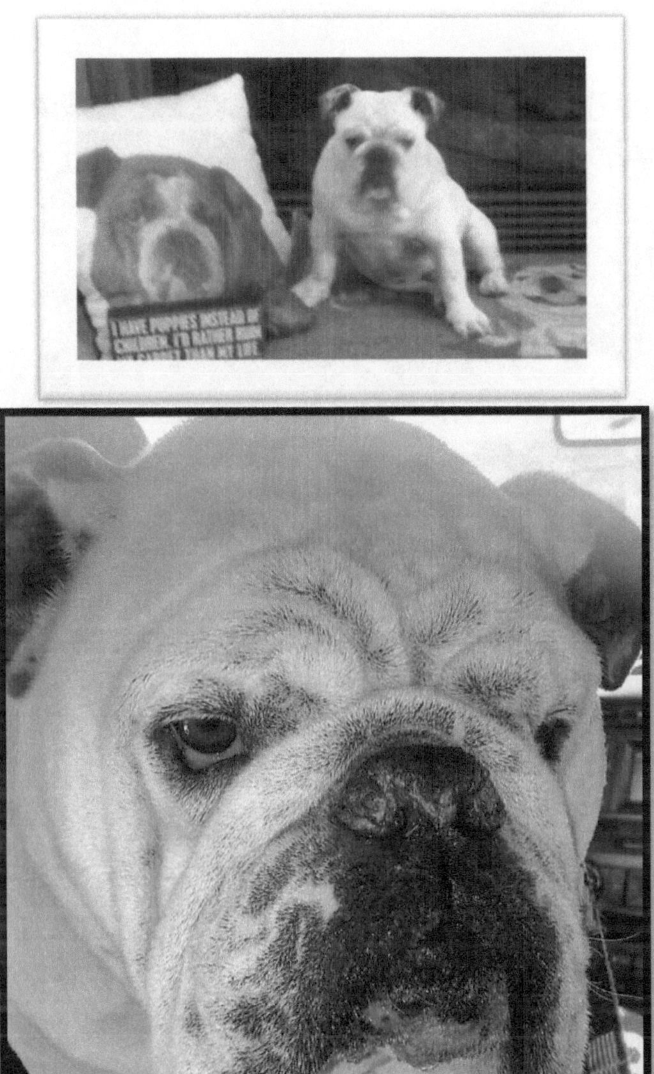

Junior- A bit older still in the same spot in his truck!

Junior with Harley

Abstract Photo "Junior" by: R .Dean

Junior in Florida Checking To See Who

Is Visiting Today!

Watch Out For Dog Kisses From Junior!

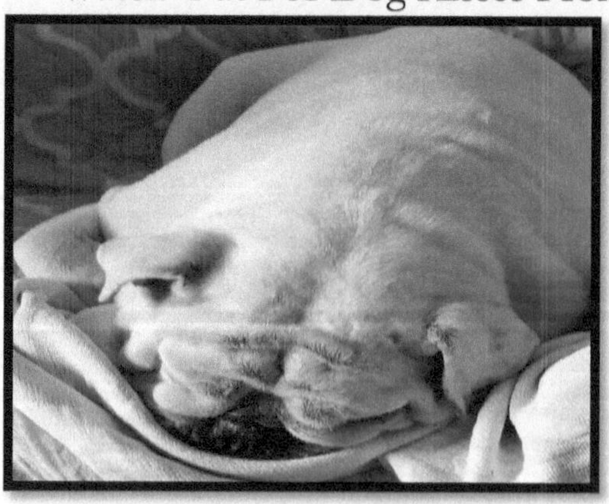

AW- NAP!

4 BOBO

Bobo was a rescue dog with a lot of health issues. They were not obvious at first. He was not used to being treated nicely and was kept in a crate for so long he didn't develop his pads on his feet. His teeth were rotten and he was almost blind in one eye. No animal should have to be treated like that!

Bobo was abused for the first four years of his life. He is making up for lost time now with his buddy Junior. He is an example of what can happen if you miss good nutrition in formative years. His rotten teeth were pulled. He has a cherry eye that has been surgically repaired three times since it never properly formed. The tear duct keeps popping out.

Bo is short for **Beauregard** who was Junior Sample's dog. Bo's name was Rambo when the Callahan's got him, but he never answered to that name so they changed it. He was to be company for Junior so they kept the HeeHaw tradition and named him Bo but call him Bobo. He wasn't used to being feed on a regular basis, so when he first started getting good food he gobbled it up too fast thinking

he might not get anything for a long time.
 Now he eats normally and takes his time and his very happy!
Treats are also welcomed anytime!

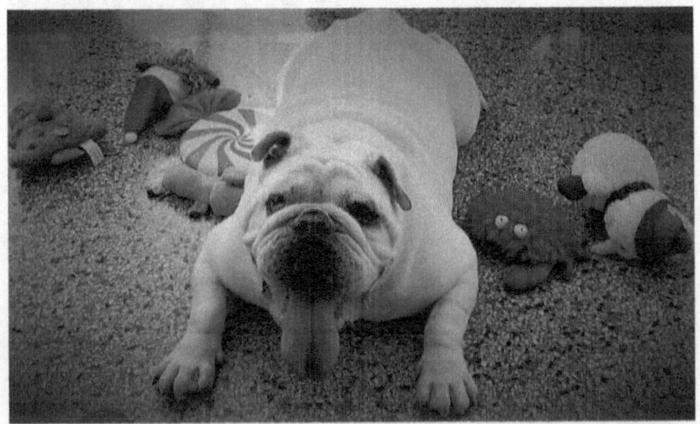

All in all, Bobo has a very nice disposition. Strangers stop and ask to pet him and he loves the attention! He now lives in a good home close to the beach in two different places so he won't have to deal with the cold weather! The two dogs coordinate the Toys For Tots Campaign every Christmas with their owners. People love to see these guys when they drop off their donations. They get pets, treats, and their pictures taken. They collected over a hundred bicycles for kids just last year. They love their job!

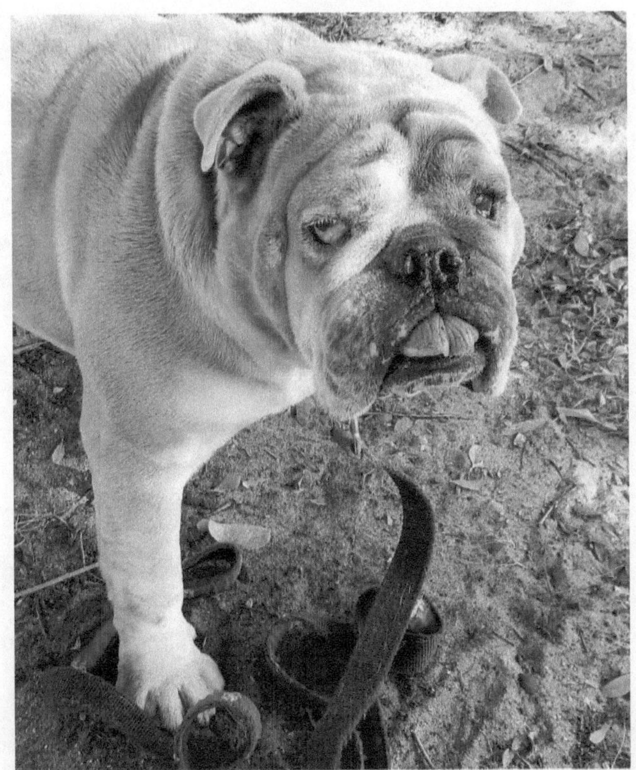

Bobo Getting Into The Dirt

Bobo looks like the classic Bulldog with the wide shoulders and the typical Marine Mascot!

Bobo

Notice the Cherry Eye on the Right!

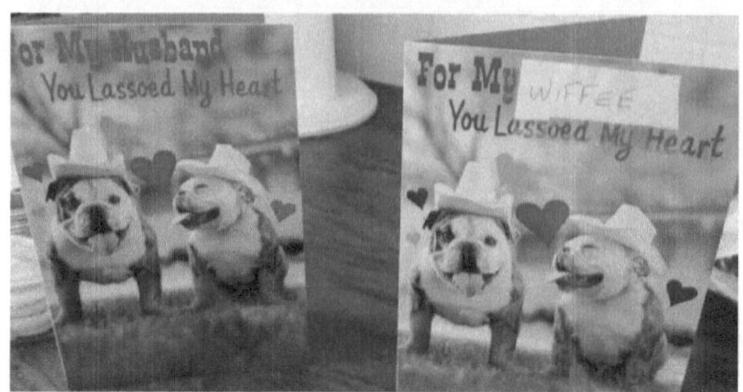

Bulldogs cards are everywhere and can be found for any occasion.

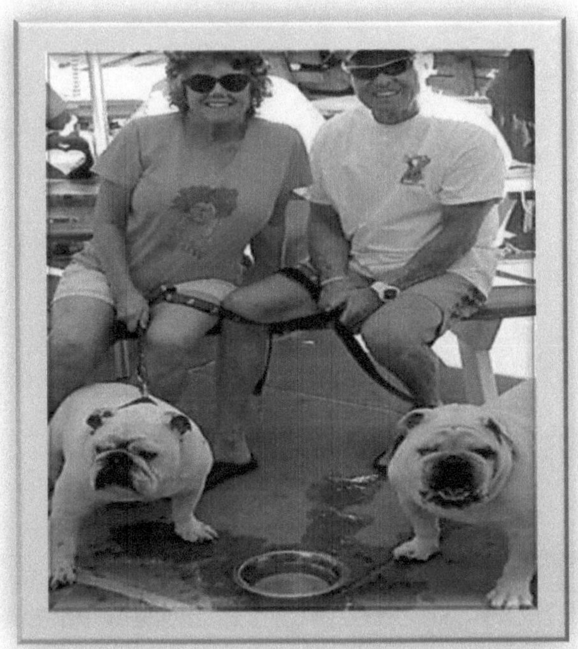

**Stopping for a drink of water after a
Long or short walk is a necessity!
Pancakes are a Sunday Treat
in Florida!**

5. BETHANY BEACH, DELAWARE

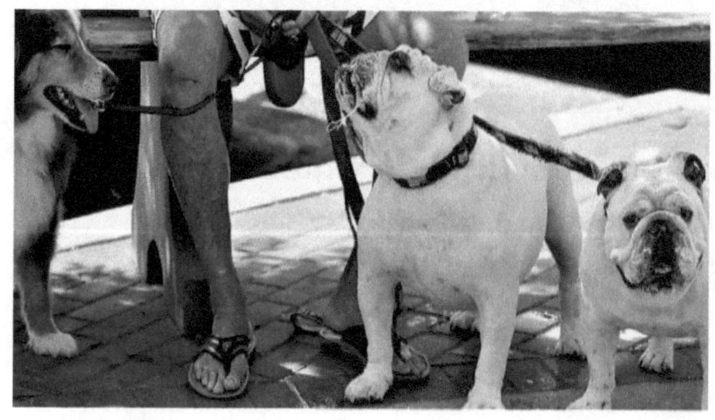

The dogs take a daily walk out by the beach where all the shops are. People come from all over and are very dog friendly. Whenever they stop, the dogs get greeted and petted and told how adorable they are! The most common questions are: What are their names? How old are they? What kind of Bulldogs are they? Etc.etc. You almost need a recorded version since they same questions are asked over and over daily, weekly, monthly and seasonal!

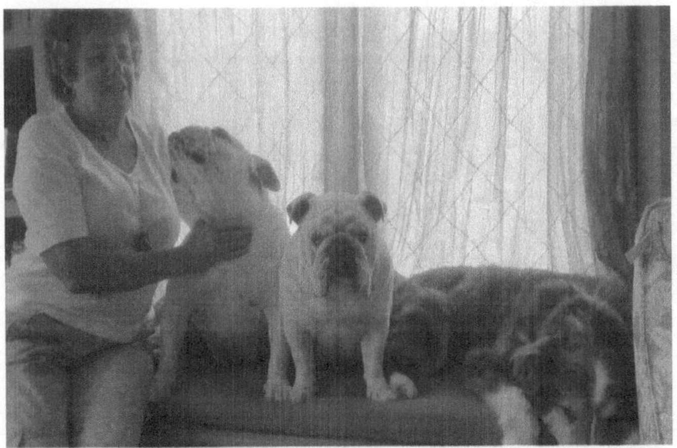

The beach house in Bethany is always full of visitors. The Bulldogs love having visitors. Harley usually is there a few times each summer season.

Bethany Beach House Favorite Dog Spot

Beach Bulldogs

YUPPY PUPPY

Bobo and Junior's Favorite place to get treats
in Bethany Beach, Delaware

Yum!

Bobo and Classic Tongue-

Photo by Roxanne Dean

7. ST.PETE'S BEACH, FLORIDA

IF IT'S HOT, TAKE A NAP, IF IT'S COOL,
TAKE A NAP, IF IT'S MORNING, TAKE A NAP,
IF IT'S EVENING TAKE A NAP

CAUTION: TOO MANY NAPS MAKE YOU AN
ACREDITED COUCH POTATO!

HOWEVER, VARYING THE POSES MAKES IT AN
AEROBIC SPORT- THUS YOU ARE GETTING
EXERCISES: LEG LIFTS, NOSE PRESSES AND
RUMP STRETCHES KEEP YOU IN GREAT SHAPE!
DON'T FORGET THE EAR FLAPPING AND THE
SNORING.
IN FLORIDA THE DOGS GET INTO THEIR TRUCK
AND DRIVE TO PASSE-A-GRILLE, A TOWN
CLOSE BY SO THEY CAN SEE THE OCEAN AND
STOP AT THE LOCAL PLACES FOR THEIR
TREATS.

THEY WALK AROUND THE BLOCK, VISIT WITH
THE DAILY WALKERS AND SHOPKEEPERS,
THEN GET BACK INTO THE TRUCK AND HEAD
HOME. THEY CAN SIT OUT IN THEIR FRONT

PORCH , INSIDE A WHITE GATE AND CATCH UP ON THEIR NAPS!

PASSING GAS IS PART OF THE DAILY WORKOUT ALSO.

JUNIOR AND BOBO CAN ALWAYS COME UP WITH A NEW WAY TO FIT ON THE COUCH EFFECTIVELY.

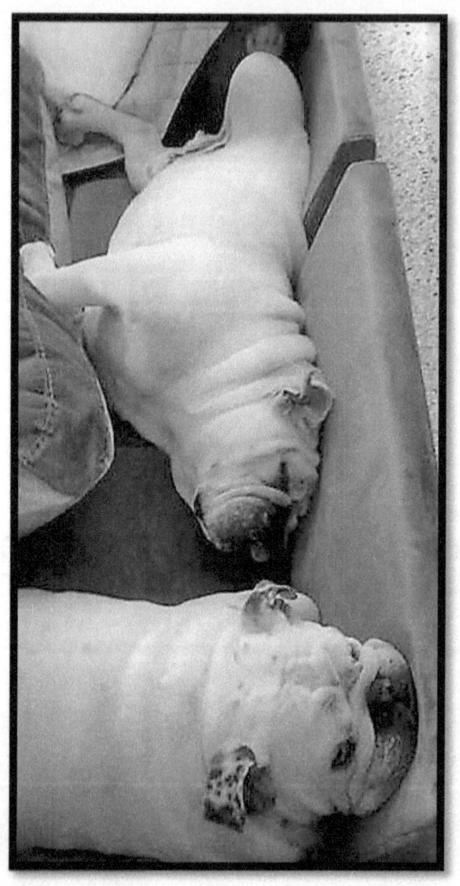

BOBO LOVES HIS TOYS

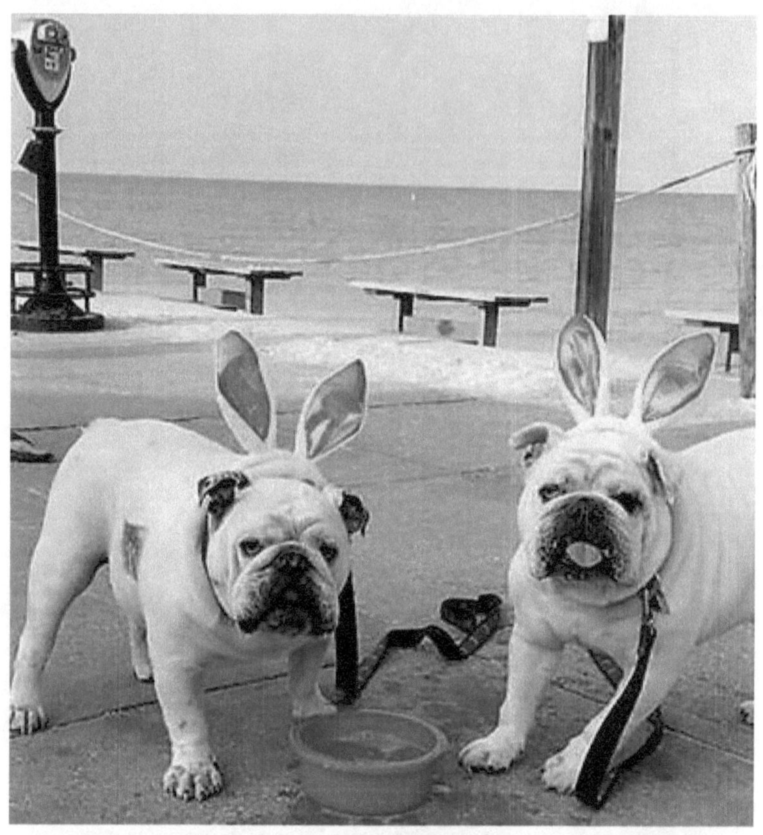

FLORIDA WALK IN Pass-a-Grille Beach
(Easter Ears)

Florida Sights While Walking

FOOD FIGHT

FLORIDA BIRDS

HOLIDAY FASHIONS

7. 

Junior and Bobo are visited quite frequently by neighbors and relatives. Harley an Australian Shepherd is a cousin(family relation) and sometimes stays with them in the summer at their Bethany Beach Home in Delaware. He gets to enjoy Doggie Ice cream when he is there.

Gma visits while Junior and Bobo get a spot on the ends of the couch.

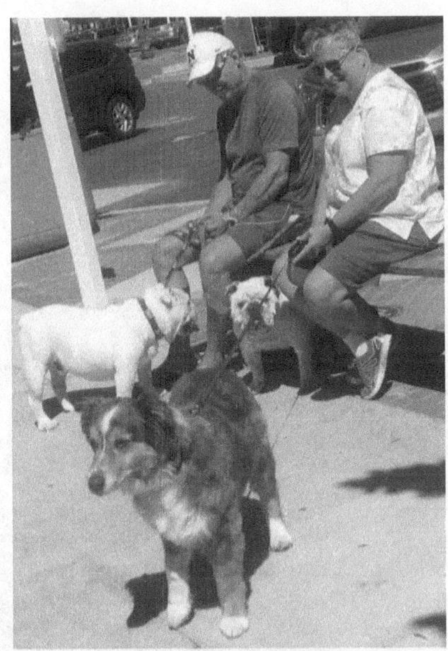

The Dogs Love It When **Sally** Walks Them!

One of the biggest fans of the dogs is their neighbor Sally who lives down the other side of Lake Bethany. She became friends with the whole family and loves to help walk the dogs. Sally's favorite is BOBO, they get along so well and they are frequently seen hanging out by the beach. They go to the shops that give out dog treats and water almost daily during the summer season until they close in October. The "Yuppy Puppy" is one of their favorite places to visit.

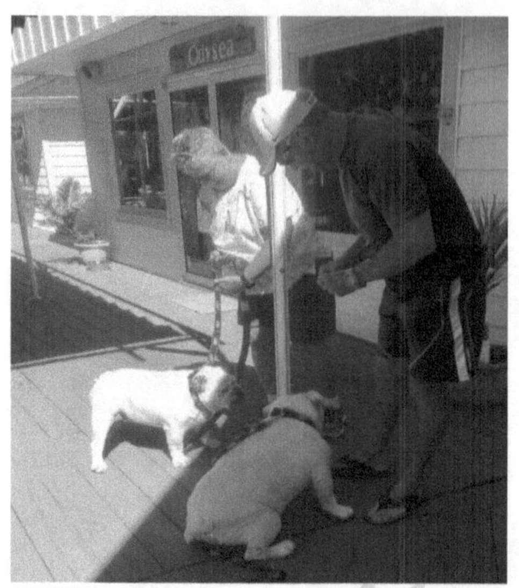

Details

Bulldogs Have Wrinkles, Bulldogs can stare
Bulldogs can leave many farts in the air!
Bulldogs don't hurry, they really don't care
They'll look at you like you're the one needing
the chair.
Bulldogs are funny, they can be comical
As long as we laugh quite astronomical.
Bulldogs like treats, they don't have a limit
They'll eat all that you give them- all that is
permitted!

Bulldogs are cute, they are lovable creatures
They come as a package with lots of neat

features!

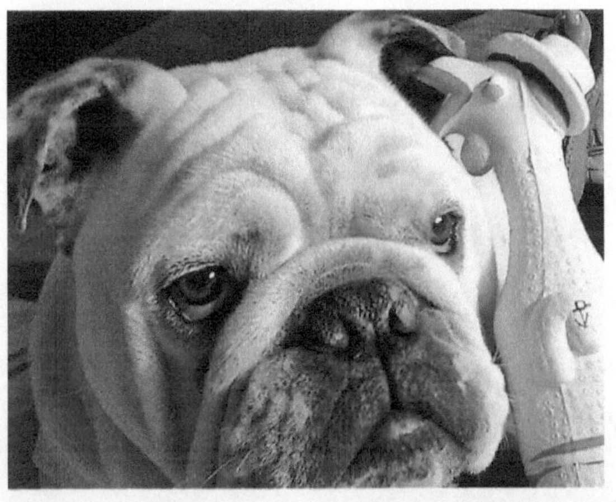

Bobo Thinking About Attacking This Toy!

8.

Cartoon Characters of Bulldogs

Hector the Bulldog

Hector the Bulldog -
en.wikipedia.org › wiki › Hector_the_Bulldog

Hector the Bulldog is an animated cartoon character in the Warner Bros. Looney Tunes and Merrie Melodies series of cartoons. Hector is a muscle-bound bulldog with gray fur (except in "A Street Cat Named Sylvester" and "Greedy for Tweety", where his fur is yellowish) and walks pigeon-toed.

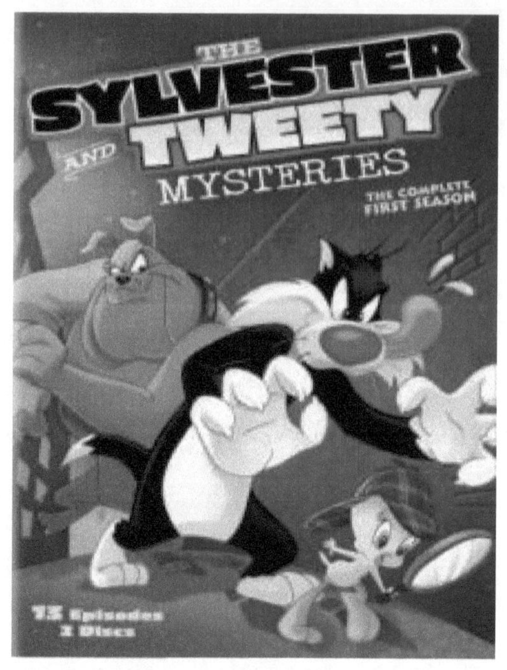
THE
SYLVESTER
AND TWEETY
MYSTERIES
THE COMPLETE
FIRST SEASON
13 Episodes
3 Discs

Spike Bulldog is a gray, rough bulldog that appears in many of Tom and Jerry cartoons. He has a somewhat minor friendship with

Jerry and is a formidable enemy.

Spike the Bulldog and Chester the Terrier are animated cartoon characters in the Warner Bros. Looney Tunes and Merrie Melodies series of cartoons. Spike is a burly, gray bulldog who wears a red sweater, a brown bowler hat, and a perpetual scow

Spike the Bulldog

Similar Dog Cartoons

Droopy

Droopy is an animated cartoon character from the Golden Age of American Animation: an anthropomorphic dog with a droopy face, hence the name Droopy. He was created in 1943 by Tex Avery for theatrical cartoon shorts produced by the Metro-Goldwyn-Mayer cartoon studio. Essentially the polar opposite of Avery's other famous MGM character, the loud and wacky Screwy Squirrel, Droopy moves slowly and lethargically, speaks in a jowly monotone voice, and—though hardly an imposing character—is shrewd enough to outwit his enemies. When finally roused to anger, often by a bad guy laughing heartily at him, Droopy is capable of beating adversaries many times his size with a comical thrashing ("You know what? That makes me mad!").

featuring MGM's other famous cartoon stars, Tom and Jerry.

In the cartoon Northwest Hounded Police, Droopy's last name was given as "McPoodle". In The Chump Champ, it was given as "Poodle". Nevertheless, Droopy is generally understood to be a basset hound.

History
Metro-Goldwyn-Mayer
Character information

Nationality

American
Quote

"Hello, all you happy people."

Droopy is an animated cartoon character from the Golden Age of American Animation: an anthropomorphic dog with a droopy face, hence the name Droopy. He was created in 1943 by Tex Avery for theatrical cartoon shorts produced by the Metro-Goldwyn-Mayer cartoon studio.

There are many rescue sights and Bulldog Forum News that also give the titles of all the movies that Bulldogs were starred in.

Most Popular English Bulldog Movies and TV Shows

Sherlock Holmes
UP
Space Jam
Pacific Rim
Paterson
Transformers, Revenge of the Fallen
Leatherheads
Hotel For Dogs
Something Wild
Mr.MAGOO
The Scribbler
Higher Than A Kite
Flat Foot Stooges
Feeding Mr.Baldwin
Surfin Bulldog

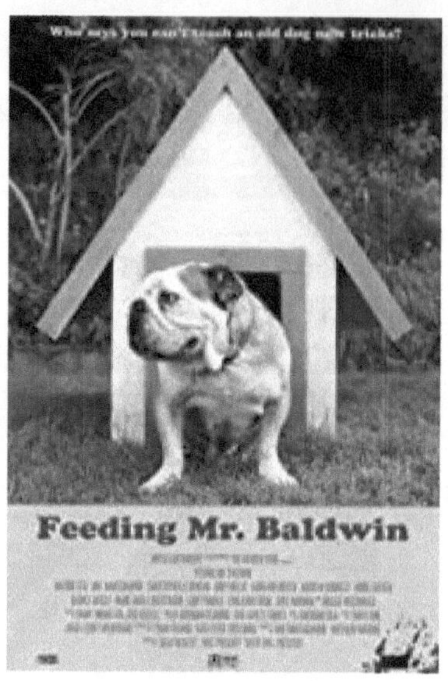

9. BULLDOG RESCUES

Organizations with English Bulldogs

- Southern California **Bulldog Rescue** Santa Ana, CA. (30) See Pets.
- Lone Star **Bulldog** Club **Rescue** McKinney, TX. (47) See Pets.
- Illinois **English Bulldog Rescue** Decatur, IL. (7) See Pets.
- Chicago **English Bulldog Rescue** Park Ridge, IL. (6) See Pets.
- Florida **English Bulldog Rescue** Odessa, FL.

Bulldog Rescues

https://www.facebook.com/Bravobulldogs123/

https://www.rescuebulldogs.org/

https://rescuebulldogs.wordpress.com/

Hillplace Bulldogs guide to buying a bulldog puppy - YouTube

How can I tell if my English bulldog is purebred?

What is the most popular English bulldog color?

Buying A Bulldog The Definitive Guide - Castlewood Bulldogs

www.castlewoodbulldogs.com › buying-a-bulldog-the-...

1.

English bulldogs are the mascots of choice for many colleges, organizations, and even ... Below are some tips on how to shop and buy a Bulldog **puppy**, what to look for in a ... I found a great a Breeder how **do I choose** a dog that's **right** for me?

We'll Tell You What to Look for When Buying a Bulldog Puppy ...

petponder.com › Dogs

1.

Bulldogs—French or **English**—are very adorable and cute

How to choose the right English bulldog puppy – Blue Mountain

bluemountainbulldogs.com ›

Jun 7, 2019 - We can get into why they are so expensive later, but for the purpose of this article suffice it to say that **getting** a **bulldog puppy** represents a ...

How to Choose an English Bulldog - Euro Puppy

www.europuppy.com › Blog

Jul 12, 2010 - This is not to say that **getting** an **English Bulldog** guarantees you will face serious ... Bulldogs are **best** suited to temperate climates and not very ...

Things you need to know before you buy a English Bulldog

Main things to look for when buying an English Bulldog ...

bulldogbackyard.com › Adoption

1.

Sep 13, 2018 - One of the **best** ways to get an ideal sized **Bulldog** is observe the parents when working ... No one wants to have a **puppy** that is not healthy.

What You Need To Know In Selecting English Bulldog Puppies |

www.englishbulldoginformation.org › english-bulldog-...

How to choosing the best English bulldog puppies for you that is not only healthy but complements your personality for a more harmonious and quality way of ...

A Guide to English Bulldogs: Puppies, Temperament, Diet ...

pethelpful.com › Dogs › Breeds

Aug 21, 2019 - The **English Bulldog** has been a popular breed since the late 1800s and was initially bred for ferocity and courage. ... If you are still wondering if the Bulldog is **right** for you, then the **best** place to ... **Choosing** Your First **Puppy**.

7 Things To Consider Before Buying A Bulldog - 11 Best Dog ...

dogstrollersreviews.com › bulldog › 7-things-to-consid...

You can buy an **English Bulldog** or French Bulldog. Cute Bulldog **puppy** ... For **selecting** the **pet** you have to check the characteristic of the dog. **Buying** a Bulldog ...

Images for how to pick the right english bulldog puppy

Rescue Dogs Get Dressed For Special Ocassions!

Junior and Bobo Enjoy A Sip of Guinness on St. Patrick's Day

Ode To Junior and Bobo

Junior and Bobo are Bulldogs in white
They have special markings that
Enriches their life!
They stroll down the street at a slow pace-
Not a hurry! In fact that is rare to see
Them move quickly, they don't scurry!
Their heads bob along as they check out
the scents. They calculate new visitors
who come down and pay rent.
They each have their spots that they go for
deposits. Doggie bags have to follow this
routine- there are wallops.
Tourists navigate to wherever they are,
They have this down pat, they enjoy being
the star!

Leopard spots on Junior's ears became
quite the attraction. Bobo gets comments
on his classic size and compaction!
Just give them a treat, not just one, you
need more. Otherwise they will get some at
the local pet store.

Soon back to the truck since it's time to
get home. Doggie ice cream will follow
some dinner at their dome.
Then time for some fun with toys that can
squeak, the scene that will follow is not for
the meek!
Aw -time to squeeze next to the people
they love- for this is when they get all
snuggly and rubbed.
Bedtime rolls around and they look for their
beds, so when morning has broken they
can stretch out those legs!

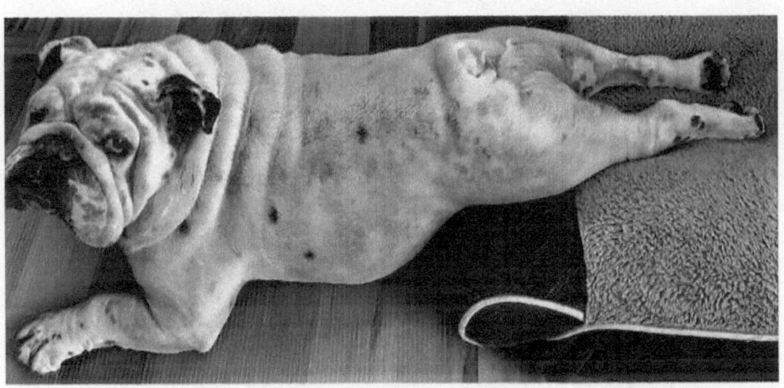

Some of Roxanne's Photography Awards

Bobo

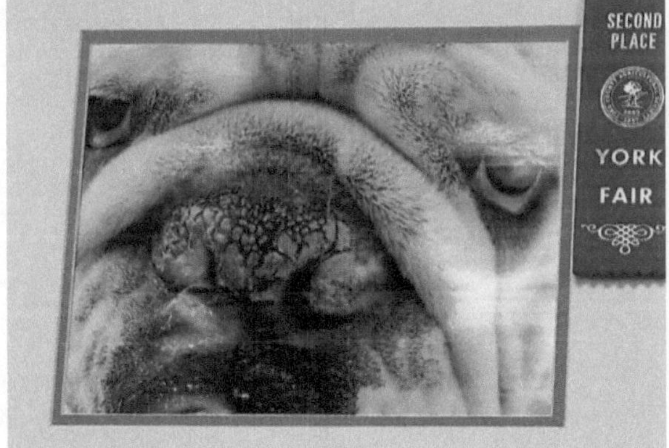

Junior

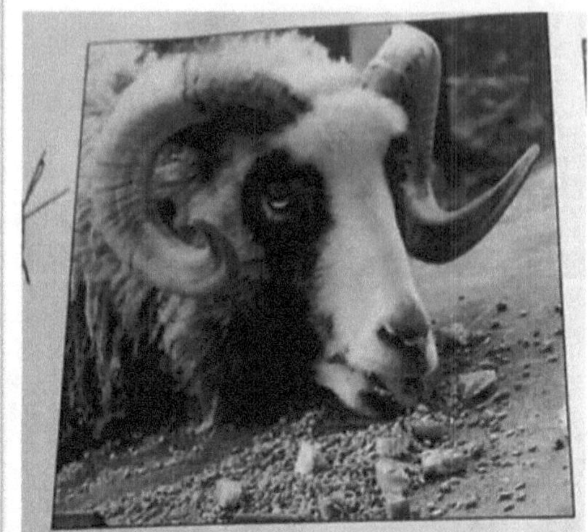

"Yum!" by Roxanne Dean of Celtic Herd
Farm, in Glen Rock, Pennsylvania.

still filled with all the curiosity of bums
(bottle lambs). Enjoy it while it lasts!
Now this next image is certainly an
unusual sight! It's "Laggy Tongue"
and he likes to lick up apple slices and
"grainola" from flat surfaces, not frozen
cast iron please! Naming sheep? It's bes

10. ABOUT THE AUTHOR
ROXANNE DEAN

Roxanne is an animal lover and raises Scottish Sheep in Glen Rock, Pa. She has published ten other books about animals. The first book: "The Sheep of Celtic Herd," is a (ewemorous) story from the point of view of the sheep and has gotten many laughs from all ages. She has an Australian Shepherd, "Harley" who has three books out about him and one about another Bulldog named "Lenny". They all include fiction and non-fiction and are appropriate for ages 8 up to adult. All photographs are her original photos. Many of the photos have won awards in many different categories. The books are all available on Amazon books and Kindle.

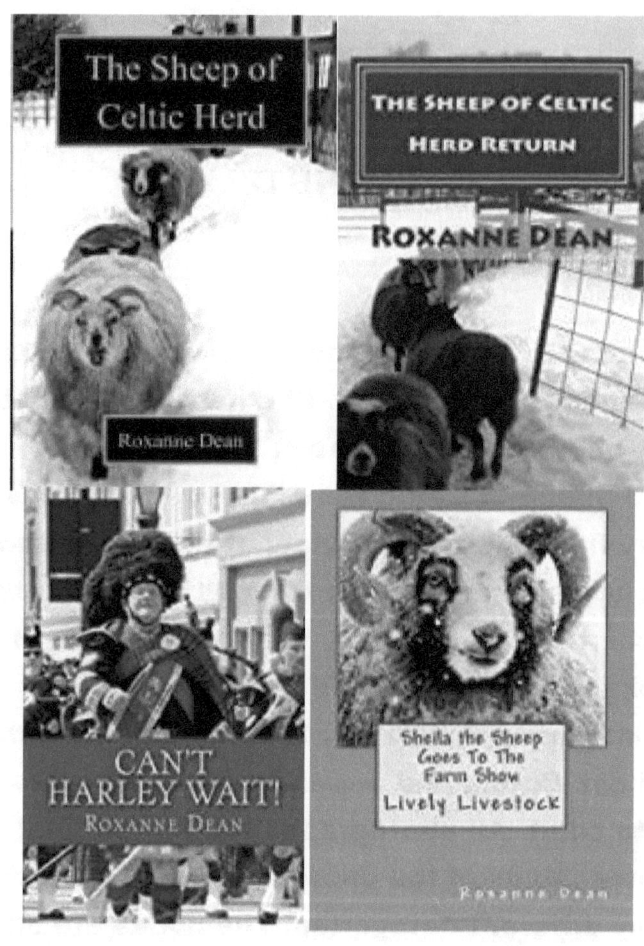
The Sheep of
Celtic Herd
Roxanne Dean

THE SHEEP OF CELTIC
HERD RETURN
ROXANNE DEAN

CAN'T
HARLEY WAIT!
ROXANNE DEAN

Sheila the Sheep
Goes To The
Farm Show
Lively Livestock
Roxanne Dean

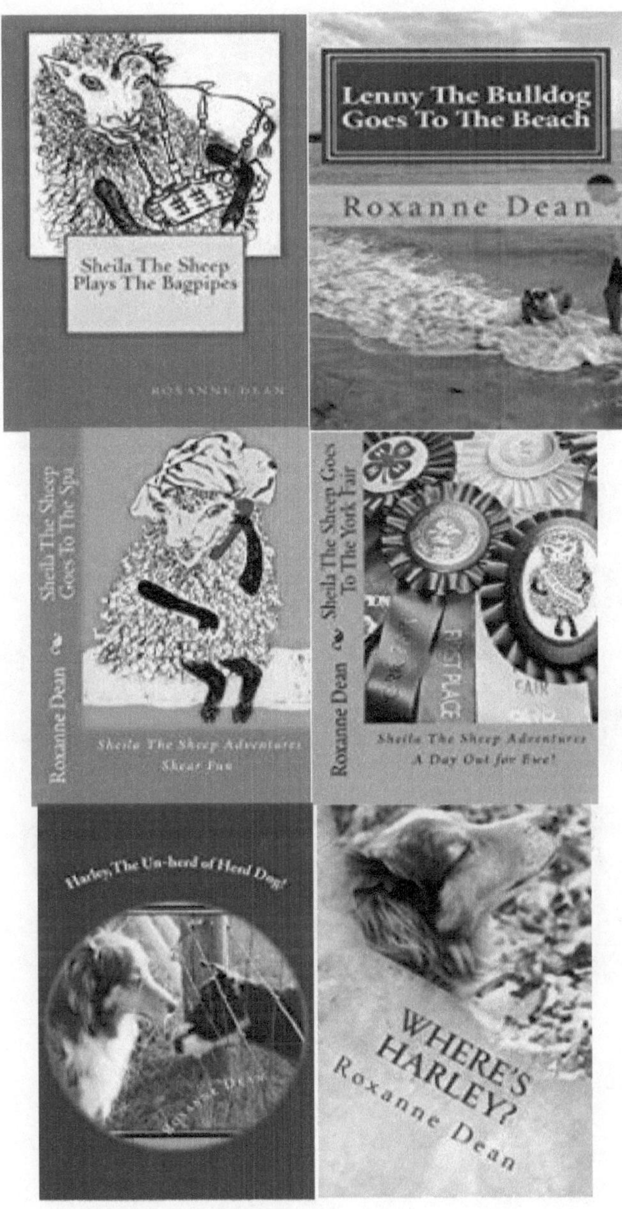
Sheila The Sheep
Plays The Bagpipes
ROXANNE DEAN
Lenny The Bulldog
Goes To The Beach
Roxanne Dean
Sheila The Sheep
Goes To The Spa
Roxanne Dean
Sheila The Sheep Adventures
Shear Fun
Sheila The Sheep Goes
To The York Fair
Roxanne Dean
Sheila The Sheep Adventures
A Day Out for Ewe!
Harley The Un-herd of Herd Dog!
WHERE'S
HARLEY?
Roxanne Dean

TODAY IS MY LAZY DAY
PLEASE DON'T ASK ME TO
MOVE IT IS
COUNTERPRODUCTIVE TO
MY CURRENT GOALS
www.febr.org

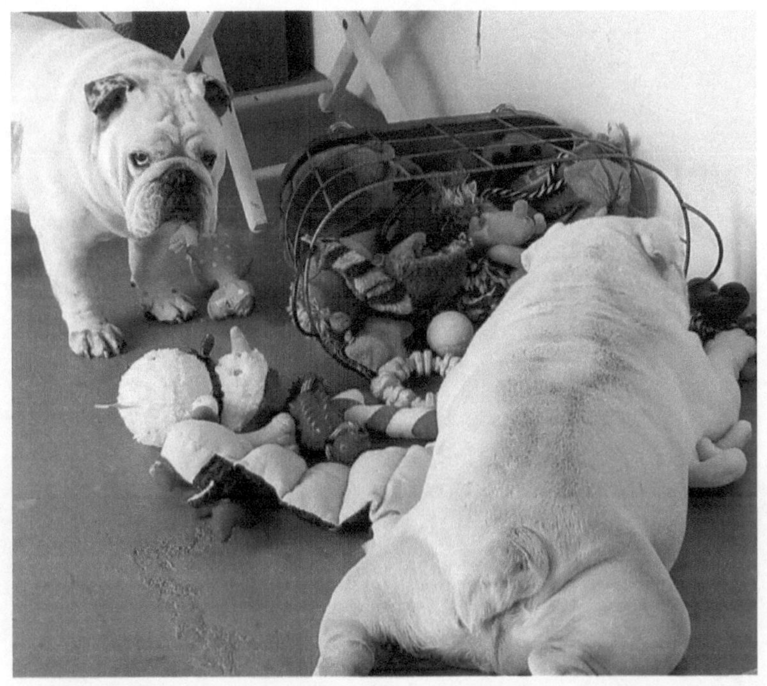

Toys! Don't Leave Home Without Them!

The Beginning......